Quiet Kid

*Winner of the 2019
Mark Ritzenhein Emerging Poet Award*

poems by

Grace Carras

Finishing Line Press
Georgetown, Kentucky

Quiet Kid

ACKNOWLEDGMENTS

Poetry Leaves Exhibition and Bound Volume "When He Tells You He Loves
You," 2019
Lansing Sidewalk Poetry Competition "for the poets who gather here" 2018
CUPSI Semifinals "For The Quiet Kids Who've Been Told Speak Up" 2018
Oakland Arts Review "She Eats" 2017

This is for my parents, Stephen and Kristina Carras.
My mentors and dear friends, Laurie Hollinger,
Ruelaine Stokes, and Dennis Hinrichsen.
Mary Fox, Rosalie Sanara Petrouske, and Mary Anna Scenga-Krunch, in
thanks for the care they took in copy-editing this manuscript, and for their
patient guidance in helping me navigate the publishing process for the first
time.
Everyone who has ever struggled to feel listened to, and for everyone who isn't
sure if it ever gets easier. It does.

Publisher: Leah Maines
Editor: Christen Kincaid
Cover Art: Created by ngupakarti - pngtree.com
Author Photo: Christopher Bakken
Cover Design: Elizabeth Maines McCleavy

Order online: www.finishinglinepress.com
also available on amazon.com

Author inquiries and mail orders:
Finishing Line Press
P. O. Box 1626
Georgetown, Kentucky 40324
U. S. A.

Table of Contents

reintroduction

find me in the corner of the park with the
flowers and the frothing crush of people

you can follow the paper trail
the one lined with jitterbugs and

gingerbread and residue
of fog

i will be there
waiting with the poem you wanted

(not this one)
you can dig

through the bags in my eyes for it
it's in me somewhere

for the quiet kids who have been told Speak Up

remember
thunder doesn't care who hears it

next time someone tells you to Speak Up
Quiet Kid
say this is my voice
just like yours it is a storm

this is no punchline
this is not silence

remember the days you went without speaking at all
when you wore Quiet like a shadow
when you wore Quiet like a name
when Quiet was your name

those days you became the word absence
when you learned to hate the sound of your own laugh
for the way it uncrumples in the air
creeps

like weeds and bruises
how it sounds like mold
Quiet Kid this

is not silence
next time someone says Speak Up
ask them
how many people do you know with a voice like lightning?
can you see the fire in my mouth?
can you see how much of me is burning?

you know the answer
you know that there's no sound in space
and that's still where stars explode

you have always been supernova Quiet Kid
next time they say Speak Up say

listen

excerpts of voicemails from lovers or exes

After Doc Luben

1. The sex was great.

2. You know me better than this—I'm not squishy. This has never been something I've known how to articulate.

3. Keep the jacket; it looks better on you. There are other things I'd like to give you. I think you can imagine what some of them are.

4. You remind me of black coffee, and the smell of chlorine, and that time in 10th grade when Ashton slapped me across the face.

5. My great-grandfather wanted to wear bright orange and purple suits to business meetings, but he was alive in the 1940's, when everyone hated fun. So, he would sew colorful patches of silk cloth onto the insides of all of his sportcoats. Every day, he would carry rainbows against his ribs. I can't imagine a better secret. I can't imagine love looking like anything else.

6. When I was 10 years old, I found a duck egg by the lake. I wrapped it in wool, even sat on it, waited for something to hatch. Of course it didn't. For months, I thought I'd killed it. I didn't know how to forgive myself for everything I wasn't able to nurture.

7. When I try to talk to you, it feels like something is plucking words and sounds from my throat before they can reach my tongue. I can't stop slurring. I feel like a drunk, constantly fumbling for my own voice.

8. This feels like being taken apart. I am disassembled. If you looked, I'm sure you could find spare pieces of me under your bed, in your closet, in the trash next to the toilet. This has been such a long time coming.

9. You've already told me that I apologize too much; I hope you're proud of me when I tell you that I have never been less sorry than I am right now.

10. You left the bathroom lights on again. You forgot to feed the fish. At least try to remember your coat when you leave. It's going to be cold.

you thought i wasn't listening, and i wasn't

because i was watching. you were

cutting onions
and not exactly
crying, but
i could see the redness
in your eyes
and the gleaming reflection
of the kitchen.

when i think no
one is looking, i stand
in front of the mirror
and speak to no one in voices
that aren't mine.
or maybe they are mine,
and they just don't know it yet
or maybe i am theirs,
and i just haven't gotten comfortable,

and maybe that's why i don't often
call you by your name and why
i don't utter my own much, either.
because it sounds
like a stranger naming me or worse,
a stranger naming you, and
here's the thing:
my naked voice feels so wild to me,
i worry that it will choke
the love from anything
i ask it to hold.

but the way you look up
from your knife
tears winking from the edges
of your smile lines
ask if i'm paying attention
without correcting myself, i think *yes,
how comfortable this is.*
for a moment i forgot i was here.
for a moment it was just you.
but i don't say that.
i tell you i was thinking
about how good you look.
and that redness turns

just a little more pink
and now it doesn't matter
what our voices sound like
or who's almost crying.
there is no more
use for words or tears.

this, this

after "This, This" by Mahogany L. Brown

this trouble
this tug and rip of skin
this skin more place than skin
this skin made map to nowhere
this overarch
this ligament turned bubblegum
this Big League Chew
this gnashing heat
this heat
this stovetop palm
   flaming throat
   eruption of smoke
   fevering together
this volcanic breath
this place
this landscape with
this twist and turn
this turning into
this something
   something that becomes
this unfolding of the lungs
   butterfly of insides
this almost beast
this Trouble
this big bad wolf
   snake in the garden

this villainous cliché
this chase
this stay
this pound of pulse
this roaring motion in
this still body
this motion its own song
this song its own body
   more map than music
this body still
this body
this here now
this body
this one
   with the world inside

haibun: the meadow

It was there, in the copper light, when he turned around to face me and smiled, that the way back to my parent's house blipped out of existence. He smiled like he had a mouthful of holy water; he looked, in that moment, like the type of man who would never ever raise his voice. We had been picking juniper berries and the needles bit our fingers and I was bleeding, and in that moment, there was no such thing as depression or distance or doubt, no tightrope tension between family and him, and I was, very suddenly, no longer a disappointment. And dinner was starting soon, so we needed to drift back out of the meadow, along the dirt bike trail, across the river, back to my parent's house, but, in that moment, like I said, the way back had ceased to be. There was only that smile, his hair curled like a question mark inside his hat, his smell of grease and cloves and woodsmoke and semen hanging thick from his body, and it was the smile of someone who had never in his life felt ugly. And there I was,

bleeding from my fingers,
my hands drooling at the sight
of him.

crush

i'm still holding myself up to the light
looking for the false bottom on my memory
wondering where she hid the switch
to the trap door of my confidence
i loved her from
the back of the class
quiet as dust
so caught in the pull of all her heavy
that i never actually spoke a word to her
it was such young love
that i gave her baby's breath instead of roses
in all of my daydreams

she had a smile that devoured
a black hole laugh
this hair
galactic
huge

and
her hands
magician-like
something in the movement of them
like she was full of rabbits and glitter

we were in high school
it was probably nothing
but enough nothing at some point
becomes so so much
black holes carry worlds inside
we are sixteen years old for ages
there is nothing more human than time
there is nothing like loving someone
who turns your lungs into acrobats
who invents her own gravity
young love is just a limb of the beast of inspiration
i am still there behind the teeth of

this wizard girl
this lipsticked milky way
flying and falling sound the same in the ears
only the chest knows which way is up

epithalamium

a song or poem celebrating a marriage.

If I'm the dog fart, then you are the hot car that contains me.
I'm the dead goldfish, and you are every clogged toilet.
I'm the sex scene in the PG-13 movie,
and you are, of course, the parents.
My dearest darling darling dear,
with every pair of white shorts comes
a bloodstain;
with every sext comes
a Read Receipt from Mom at 6:27pm.
That is to say,
we belong together like
disasters and bad timing;
wherever you go, I will follow to make sure
that if anything's going to crash,
it's also going to burn.

when he tells you he loves you,

and you find you cannot say it back,
you'll feel your nerves begin to curl
inside your limbs like ferns
in the bonfire. There will be

that gaping silence.
The silence will feel like the gnawing of baby teeth;
that methodical chew that learns and identifies and names.
It will, probably, name you
awkward. You will expect your tongue to shrivel
there, go hard and wrinkled in your mouth
like a peach pit. But no.
Love is not the kind of warmth that spoils milk
or melts pumpkins like candle wax.
Regardless of all of the things you find you cannot say,
you will remain pink in all of the places you were pink before.

You will continue to cycle that ebb and flow of spit
and breath and sweat and you will say other things.
And the boy, when he understands
you do not love him, will be mostly fine.
Our egos are wet, crumbling sand castles that harden
for a moment any time someone tells us we remind them
of a good song or a superhero. Meaning,
you are intimate, like the perfect
handshake. There is no darkness
like the one between the palms. It is not love.
But it is warm air and that same gravity, and there, in that
echo chamber of bodies, the silence will name you

tangled as the highways; curling
always, around and around, in the ever-changing
direction of light.

for the poets who gather here

with thanks to The Poetry Room and The Robin Theatre

this is for you,
who overcome the trembling
dance of your own pulse
to blossom in the stage light.
you, who dig your roots in deep
and sprout from rock bottom.
go forth and devour, you
conquerors of concrete,
who put the we in weeds,
you brilliant bouquets of breath;
i've seen you carry explosions
in your mouths.
you hungry poets,
i'm in love
with the shrapnel of your bravery,
with the way you become the light
that you need to grow.

sentinels

after Tim Seibles' "Renegades"

we   always have   always will
fidget
we fidget like   June
like swimmer's itch
like light in rubies

we   fidget like swollen zits
we fidget like stars and
birch trees   and   coral
they say "*stop wwwwatching*"
they say "*don't   stare*"
we fidget like Phoenix   at 8pm

always   have
we fidget like country   boys
like refugees like dead elk
like   monsters
we fidget
always   will

we fidget   like worms
flooded to the sidewalk
like stadiums and stage lights
like yellow wallpaper
they say "*speakup*"
we fidget like deadlines
and ice cream and   freezing
rain

like   orange
like mouths and ears
like moldy watermelon
always have
we fidget like freezer   burn
we fidget like cobras and
skinny dippers

like   creeps
like   bears
like broken   glass
we   fidget
we   fidget
          we

an exercise in writing and editing drunk

the sky is an angry mother and a broken lightbulb
the storm does not come or pass
just exists a mile to the east
kissing us with that green wind in the darkness
here in the valley
it's all sound and no light now
where a cousin will be married next season
where a year ago someone or other
pressed a kiss to my shoulder
over a sweater and thought
i couldn't feel it
i'm with my friends now
with our juvenile selves in these tall bodies
the laughter of my brothers here might be the first sound
i've ever really heard
like the creaking of wood or perhaps teeth grinding
i melt towards dirt and the bugs crawl
over my skin like i'm an old broken statue
something to be consumed by mouths or history
and i think they know i may be both
i know we aren't the galaxy's final project
my face ultimately is for the bugs
i feel like one of them under all this thunder
under this wind
splayed out
one brother says from nowhere
you seem bear-eaten
i know it's true
i imagine my eyes are full of honey
imagine being ripped slowly apart by jawfuls
the carving away
of my thigh and my neck and my wrist
become blood and dirt and root
windfallen phantom
haunting myself

a snapshot of my brother

when Andrew is about to laugh,
the corners of his smile fold
tight to keep the two hemispheres
of his face from cracking apart.
when the tension snaps,
Andrew's laugh is like
the hiss of a train lunging into motion,
there and then fading and then gone.

there is a photo of him
on the table in the hallway.
he's 6 years old in a yellow life jacket
and shrieking with joy, his arms thrown open
wide like the wings i've always known he had
in another life. Andrew,
Little Andrew, the gentle child.
the quiet kid. the trampoline artist,
tightrope walking on my heartstrings.
your laughter is a precious thing.
i will hold it with both hands
until it flutters off into the sky.

looking at my mother in four rooms

i.
Kristina is gentle like her father.
she strokes the dog's head,
pulls him into her lap.
their breathing is as tender as falling leaves.
other days, her voice
is wound like a coil on a trampoline.
her focus crystalizes when someone
is crying. her fingers have
wiped away tears in every room of this house.
in this one, she's held her children's heartbreak
in the palm of one hand, turned it over and over
until it crumbles through her fingers.
someone knocks a box over in the pantry
and the dog perks up and away.
she lets him go.

ii.
her favorite book right
now is *Circe* by Madeline Miller.
it puts the suns in her eyes.
she reads by the fire,
or on the couch. the light dances
in her wedding ring and in her hair.
the book is about a mother
who is also a nymph and a titan and a witch
and i know immediately why it's her favorite.

iii.
Kristina's pride
ripples outward as
she stares at a picture
of her youngest son.
he's getting his face painted at Disney.
she cradles his baby voice in her memory
and the look in her eyes is unmistakable.
her youngest son is a man now;
they both have eyes like green lights,
bodies that *go go go* and somedays
i'm waiting to watch all that energy explode
into helicoptor leaves.
outside, the lake is calm.
it rained last night.
she sinks into the memory of Disney, the smell
of face paint and sweat.

iv.
on the bathroom floor,
Kristina wipes the snot from my nose
and helps me count from one to four
and back again.
i watch, stupid with awe,
as she turns the word *mother* into action.
this shining example
breathes with me,
bright as a star,
but closer.

a portrait of my favorite color, just because

1. The depths of a scar, the color of the inside of the body.

2. Persephone's pomegranate, a sunset in hell or on mars, the bleed and splash of juice.

3. Violet watercolor exploding in a clear full glass.

4. The tongue, post-popsicle. A gradient of sugar. A valentine creeping down the throat.

5. Greek wine spilled on the white stone street. Blood-like, and not.
Hear the glass breaking? Purple crawling like weeds through the cracks.

6. The deep, dark, reddish feeling that the girl with synesthesia said was the color of my voice.

7. Lavender, shadow-like, drapes. Sunday afternoon. The rolling hum of the cat, asleep.

8. The princess dress my brother wore to a baseball game with matching clip on earrings when he was four years old. We picked lilacs and forget-me-nots, once. We've been blossoms on one daisy chain.

9. TV static, up close.

10. Shadow on concrete. Haze in the road. Autumn, dusk. I'm driving home alone. My car is quiet like the inside of the guitar in the attic. The air is purple. The smell of the neighborhood is purple. My chucks are finally falling apart after years of pounding. In my daydream, I've survived the apocalypse. I scream with joy and turn on the music. I get home safe.

thalassa

meaning: "sea" in Greek

You could
sculpt birds from
this
salt.
This is not the salt
of salt mines
or cellars.
This salt
breathes.
I saw it.
It hisses
and moans
with the voice
of the moon,
quiet and soft
as baby
hair.

This salt
kisses
the marble quarry
and the temple
ruins.
You can unfurl
your tongue
to the wind
and taste it
in
the air.
The salt
is alive.

Here.
Pluck a smooth
stone from the floor
of the Aegean,
just the size
of your finger
tip.
Put it in your mouth.
Here is your love.
Here is your body
with your body's need.

Here you are,
sucking the salt
while the salt
sucks away
at you.

old town

a tribute to Fable II*'s Bowerstone (*my all-time favorite video game)

The first thing you notice is the purple
hat on the charlatan
in the square. Mystical Murgo
slurs his r's, prods the hat (now wilting
down his forehead), tries
to sell you *a magical mirror!*
For as long as you look
into it, it will make you beautiful. Now just remember,
the magic only works if you look at it
in complete darkness.

And there is darkness here.
It precedes but does not guarantee
a storm. It droops
from the edges of buildings and the fringes
of your clothes, wet with mist.
You expect the blizzard, like a birthday,
like the relentless onset of fate.
Instead, snow seems to hang rather than fall
from that muffled sky, flakes
suspended in the air
like pieces of a giant pearl necklace,
forever shattering.

You may have been here before;
the cobblestone streets, thick and slick with grime,
remind you of your own body.
This is the place that sinks into your bones,
that you seem to recognize in cities
halfway across the world. It smells
of woodsmoke and copper and old
fish and your own cold sweat.

Murgo twirls his mustache, throws
his arms open wide
as if welcoming home
the vibrant, ringing gold of his dreams.
Someone has bought the mirror.
Bowerstone changes, like all cities do,
but you remember it the same way
forever; dismal, hushed,
grey as the whisper of wool on skin.
You carry it with you
like the cold.

she eats

"there is some shit I will not eat." –e.e. cummings

Persephone bites, scratches, and kicks all the way to Hell.
Persephone is not crushed daisies.
Persephone is brambles on fire.
Persephone feeds Tantalus and brags about it at dinner.
Persephone rolls up her sleeves, installs a fucking air conditioner.
Persephone still eats pomegranates, swallows them whole.
Persephone takes Hades to Couples Therapy.
Persephone passes the tissues, is the therapist.
Persephone wears leather in the bedroom, thrashes like she did the first day, spirals down into herself until she can see butterflies, does not mistake release for freedom.
Persephone knows freedom when she smells it.
Persephone knows freedom is the same color as envy.
Persephone fucks Hades with a strap-on, and for the first time, someone in Hell cries with pleasure.
Persephone becomes shattered wind chimes, sings in the worst weather, becomes the word Fire, becomes her mother.
Persephone never loses her howl.
Persephone never forgets how to bite.
Persephone grows out her fingernails, learns how to wield them.
Persephone is rabid dog, is lioness, takes her cage and makes it hornet's nest, Hades is never not red and purple again.
Persephone makes him the color of pomegranates.
Persephone is hellfire spit from the tongues of generations of howling women.
Persephone is the angry ghost of road kill, an explosion of glass, the black eye of a hurricane.
Persephone grows roses, wears pink, puts her makeup on like war paint, knows that it is war paint, knows that this is war, gets wine drunk, ruins Christmas, never takes another dance lesson, teaches herself.
Persephone dances.
She breathes.
She comes out alive.

alden b dow drafts a letter to frank lloyd wright about his garden

a found poem including excerpts of a letter written by Alden B Dow

~~Listen here, you old son of a bitch~~
I have chosen to plant lilies in one spot
and tulips in another. I give them both all the fertilizer
they can take and then enjoy the results.
~~It's growing season in Arizona. You'd like it~~
~~here, if you'd visit.~~
I suppose the tulip looks upon the lily as a "cheap competitor,"
but as a gardener, this idea never occurs to me.
~~We both wanted the job in Arizona.~~
~~When I got it, I thought you'd be happy.~~
I plant these flowers because they do something for me.
~~You were the first person~~
~~I wanted to tell every time success found~~
~~its winding way to my door.~~
~~Vada asks me nightly if your letter has arrived.~~
They have no thorns to prevent me from touching them.
~~May I remind you, a mentor is a brother is a friend is a precious flower.~~
The rose, with all its greatness, seems to defy
every kind of association.
~~Ask the rose; it's lonely at the top.~~
It stabs us in the fingers when we reach
to admire it and tears and slashes at any plant that tries
to grow near.
~~When I come inside, my hands~~
~~grimy with the smell of mulch, Vada~~
~~presses a palm to my hot back and her cool lips~~
~~to my cheek. She followed me to Taliesin~~
~~and back. She's founded her own school in Midland,~~
~~as I've told you. Her curriculum is revolutionary.~~
~~She's late to dinner more often than she is on time.~~
~~From Vada, I've learned that the spotlight~~
~~ebbs and flows like the tide. There is a give~~
~~and take to this. Frankly,~~
I would prize the highest and love the most,
a rose without thorns.
~~I never told you this, but Vada hated Taliesin.~~
~~The cooking classes, the hours spent embroidering this~~
~~or that. She followed me to your fellowship there~~
~~because she found joy~~
~~in my growth. Because it did something for her.~~
~~I've seen the way you looked~~
~~at your students; your barbed gaze~~
~~searching for openings, for any cracks~~

where thorns could stick. The thunderstorm
can only talk down to the weeds.
It's lonely at the top.
Listen.
Let's stop this.
When you are ready to talk, old friend,
I will be waiting in the garden.

mom friend speaks

"That one friend in your squad that's super responsible and almost over-protective of them. Usually every friend group has a mom friend, and if you think your squad doesn't have one, then you're probably the Mom Friend!" —Urban Dictionary

Mom Friend will do the math on that check.
We don't need to Google it, Mom Friend knows the way there.
Did you drink enough water? Mom Friend'll get you some.
Here, have some of Mom Friend's water.
Let Mom Friend write that down for you. We both know
you won't remember on your own.
Come on everyone, follow Mom Friend.
We're going this way now. Oh sweetie,
are you sure you want to eat that?
Mom Friend already knows what you want to order.
Mom Friend orders for you. Is that really
what you're going to wear?
We both know that's not your color
and never will be your color.
Oh, honey. You really need to ask that?
Mom Friend knows the answer, of course.
Mom Friend always knows the answer.
We both know you don't
know what you're talking about.
Oh, doll. Oh, babe. Oh, sweetheart.
See how ignorant and small you are?
See how your confidence turns its tail and runs
from Mom Friend? Because unlike someone we know,
Mom Friend is smart.
Mom Friend is long-suffering.
Mom Friend has to be here for you
so you don't get lost on your own.
Because you would be lost without Mom Friend.
You need Mom Friend.
Mom Friend keeps you humble.
Mom Friend is only saying it like it is.
Mom Friend is just being honest.
Mom Friend knows exactly how to get wherever you need to go.
Mom Friend takes your keys and drives you there.
Are you sure about that?
Are you sure that's how it works?
Are you sure that's how it happened?
We both know how bad your memory is.
Mom Friend is certainty.

Mom Friend is light in a world of rain.
Mom Friend makes sure you know where you stand.
You are the clay from which Mom Friend will shape something pretty.
Something smart. Something complete, finally.
Mom Friend is all you have.
Mom Friend is lightning tripwire.
Mom Friend is the only thing standing
between you and the storm.
Don't worry, you poor, sweet thing.
Mom Friend will swallow you whole.

bring the bass back

no one ever told me
that i could listen to music
and clean my apartment
at the same time.
here i was, thinking
that every time i feel like a bag
of smashed apples, there was no other option
but to ferment
into a cocktail of existential dread
and shame that remains, of course, both
unshaken and unstirred.

all these years
i've been putting off the getting together of my shit,
letting the dust collect
and the stink of unwashed plates
unfurl like smoke from the sink.
an object at rest stays

at rest. i didn't get it.
but where there is music,
there is dancing. where there is music,
there is a new voice in your head,
one that doesn't care if you hate yourself,
doesn't care if you need to pretend you're someone
else or somewhere else for five minutes
just to get something done. just wants
to make folks move.
i still don't know how to jumpstart
this body; how to care about home
when i don't really feel at home anywhere;
when taking a shower or peeling my fleshy,
sticky self from the bed feels monumental;

impossible. but here we go,
the runaways and etta james and betty davis
and i, a freshly-minted rockstar wearing
a shiny new daydream,
sweeping the floor,
saluting to the crowd,
lighting the candles,
hurling my body around and around the stage
like a soapy carnival ride,
opening the blinds
to let the sun in.

brash

i am not the folded hands
the sparkle of sugar on fingertips
the pink powder

you will not find the ladybug
candlelight
the ribbon coiled in me

my voice is a wild thing you
wouldn't want to hold
purple and hairy

covered in a
wet
thick

something that stinks
my fingers rip each other to confetti
there are no lilacs or lavender in my palms

on my best days, i'm
more boom
than bloom

i won't ask you to do any
peeling to find the pretty
in this fact

of my body
my ugly
the frog in me

my mismatch
is a perfect truth
like poetry

there is nothing more
beneath the surface
than this

i know i will never be an hourglass,

so i look in the mirror
and see a church window
as wide as god.

20 things i know to be true

1. Someone wrote a story about a boy whose eyes were plucked out by birds.
2. The boy's eyes were "as blue as the breaking of jars."
3. I often imagine what I would look like with blue eyes.
4. I often imagine myself as a boy.
5. I often imagine myself blind.
6. I often imagine myself as the bird.
7. I often imagine.
8. The world looks different from inside someone's mouth.
9. I envy everyone who hasn't seen it.
10. I am green like ripping paper,
            like lemon to the iris,
                  like static,
                        like

11. I have never been the screaming kind.
12. I'm the tremble, the throat filled with dead leaves,
13. I can never quite clear it.
14. My dad says I watch the ground when I walk,
15. Like I think it's going to disappear.
16. I often imagine myself blind.
17. I often imagine myself as the bird.
18. I've never fainted before.
19. But when I panic, I go blind and
            lose feeling in my arms and
                  there are pins and needles
                        and ants in me and
20. My breath is shattered glass.

why i did it

After Karin Gottshal

Because I have stood there, moonlit and naked
in the Aegean, with my palm full of sea

urchin, tender as sunshine or glass.
Because my heart is the size of a nightlight,

and my tits hang like pomegranates, and my voice
is heavy, like velvet

underwater. Because I will never have a twin sister,
because my hands will never be perfect, because

they asked me which way I swing
and I thought, *I swing the way a wrecking ball swings.*

I did it because the consequences will never scare me.
Because the last time someone called me woman,

I felt like a turtle with a painted shell,
like the shadowed smear of lipstick,

and when I'm like this, none of it matters.
I did it because it makes me feel like there might be honey

or wine flowing in my veins, like I am sweetness after all;
because when I am like this, I am Peter Pan's shadow,

a steel drum, the perfect boy band smirk. Because
they see this heaving and feel the tremour of the Earth moving.

Because my heartbeat is contagious.
Because you can look between my legs and see nothing

but treasure for miles and miles and miles.
And I know it. And I know it because I had to learn it.

And I did it because the only parts of myself I have
ever held with tenderness are my grudges.

I did it so I could say otherwise.
Here I am, saying otherwise. I'm as tender as dawn on the sea.

I did it so I could be like the moon, so
full of myself and so in love with everyone else's light

that if you didn't know better,
you'd maybe think it was mine.

to that someone within me I have no name for,

i'm picking, again, at the scab;
ripping open that same old wound
just to try to apologize, again,
for slouching

to hide these
breasts, these mountains
atop which you
have placed
your flag. but any apology
i offer is empty, thankfully,
like the mouth of a monster.
you gnash your teeth

and crunch down
on every syllable that tries
to wrangle your
unflinching
roundness; wide
as the sea.
i could learn a thing
or two
from that hunger.
isn't this how you trumpet
your own arrival?
with crash after crash? with
that pull to swallow
every shore, to speak salt
into the tongue of anyone
who insists you aren't made new
after every moonlit baptism?

they tell me,
the moon is a woman.
it isn't that i don't believe it.
i wonder what the moon
calls herself
when every other voice
melts into the wind.
the woman in me
—if there is indeed a woman in me—
is a snake eating her own tail,
which is to say,
you satisfy yourself.
you beautiful mess of puzzle.

you queer masterpiece.
i know you are also here,
in these broad
shoulders, this deep
voice. the world and i
see so little of you at
a time.

i have been
a muscled body
with ants in my hair and blood
under my fingernails.
i have been
filthy with the goop of yeast and water
and flour, the crust of my heart
thinner than the petals
of squash blossoms.
some days, i wake up
and don't know what to call
myself. every morning
i am new
because you are new.

they tell me,
when you want to apologize,
give thanks instead.
i am on your doorstep
with flowers.
i will sing for you
on the beach.
i will stand up straight
and parade you
through the sky.

someday i'll love grace carras

After "Someday I'll Love Ocean Vuong" by Ocean Vuong

Grace,
listen.

The last time you wanted to kill yourself,
you unzipped the skin
on the back of your neck
in three places with
your fingernails. The scars were massive
until they weren't anymore.
Now, whenever anyone kisses you there,
you shiver.
Don't you know
that's my favorite thing about you?

There you go again, Grace,
running through dark rooms,
not feeling for walls
or furniture, trusting that your body
gets from *a* to *b* somehow.

Before all of this is over,
you will know confidence
is not quite like that.
"Somehow" is called
sewing yourself shut
with the clothesline.
Here you are already, holding up
at the seams.
It takes guts to shake in the wind. You're
holding up.
You have always
had more wishbone than backbone.
You will still learn how to wear it.

You will still learn hope
is not turning the lights on;
hope is leaving the house.
Hope is knowing that the biggest monster
in your closet is not
you. Grace,
the most beautiful part of your body
is what it remembers.

You spend so much time
thinking about how you want to die.
This—*this*—
is how you're going to live:
with all of your shiver,
with all this regret between your teeth.
You get out of bed anyway.
You iron out this skin. Here
is the house you have haunted,
with all of its many people going
in and out
like blood and breath;
if you're going to be the fire
that brings it down,
you must also be the smoke. You also
must rush out the windows,
curl into the sky, become
blue. Some part of you
must forget the ashes.

Here you are:
shedding the caution tape.
You're gonna stop being afraid
of pill bottles and crosswalks,
stop being afraid of the things
you've wanted them to do to you.
You're gonna see
all of the pairs of eyes in this world
on the days they look more like knuckles, and
you're gonna take
this life
with all of its punches
and shake like you're dancing.
Before all of this is over, Grace,

you're gonna be fine.
you'll be fine.